GLOBETROTTERS
CHINA
Jane Hinchey
REDBACK
publishing
I0760096

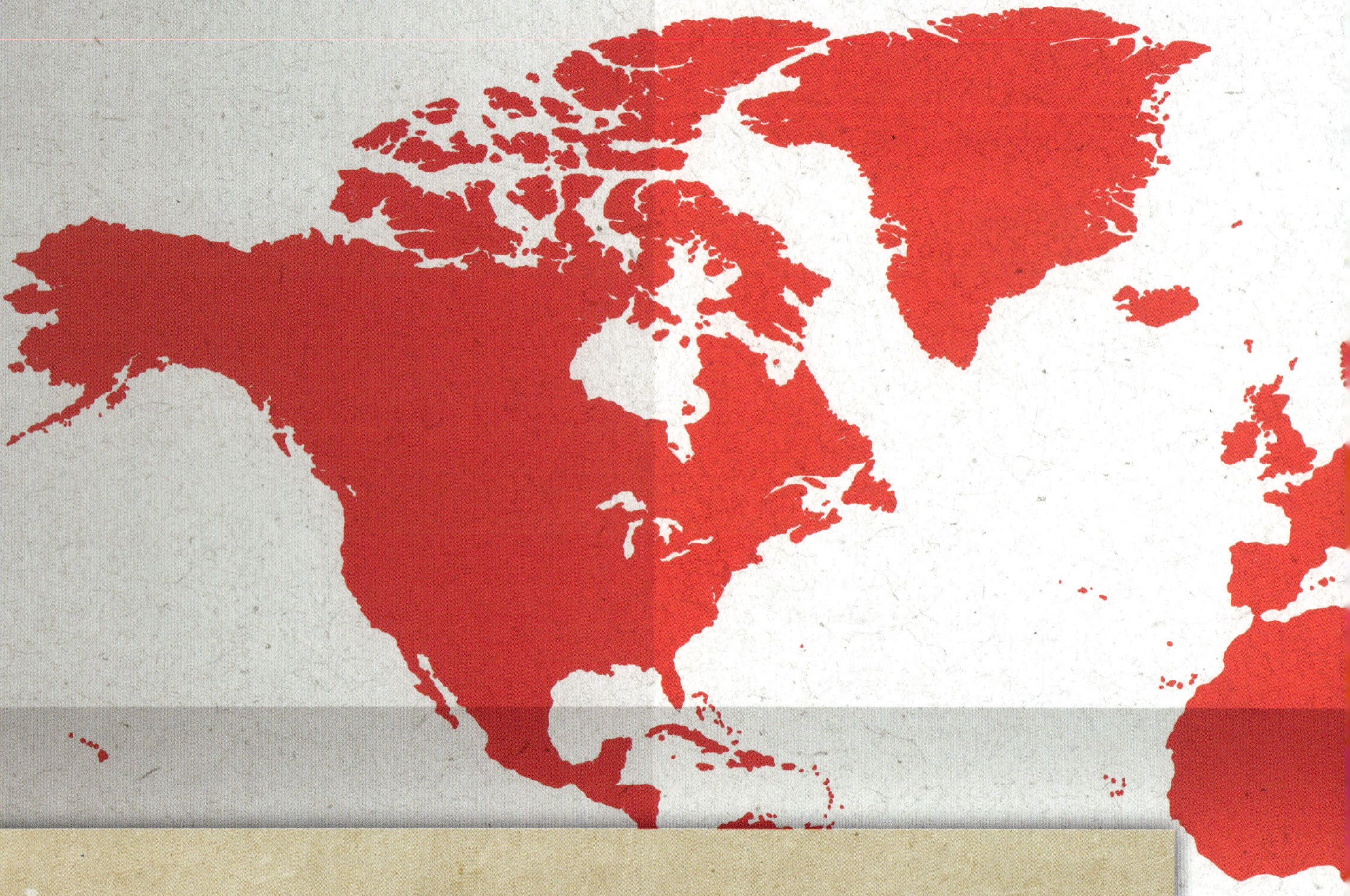

Redback Publishing
Suite 6, 13a Narabang Way,
Belrose NSW 2085
Australia

www.redbackpublishing.com
orders@redbackpublishing.com

ISBN 978-1-761401-40-4 PBK

Author: Jane Hinchey
Editor: Marlene Vaughan
Design: Redback Publishing

Original illustrations © Redback Publishing 2025
Originated by Redback Publishing

Acknowledgements
Abbreviations: l—left, r—right, b—bottom, t—top, c—centre, m—middle
We would like to thank the following for permission to reproduce photographs: (Images © shutterstock) p5tl Anton_Ivanov, p8br AleCasa77, p9br Jerome Quek, p9bl Sirio Carnevalino, p10br Weiming Xie, p11br Hung Chung Chih, p12tr LEE SNIDER PHOTO IMAGES, p12ml humphery, p13ml Tiffany Chan, p14mr SBWorldphotography, p14bl Anton_Ivanov, p16ml atiger, p16bm Jack.Q, p24cm Curioso.Photography, p24br Hung Chung Chih, p26tr Weiming Xie, p27br tangxn

Every effort has been made to contact copyright holders of any material reproduced in this book. Any omissions will be rectified in subsequent printings if notice is given to the publisher.

A catalogue record for this book is available from the National Library of Australia

CONTENTS

MAP OF CHINA

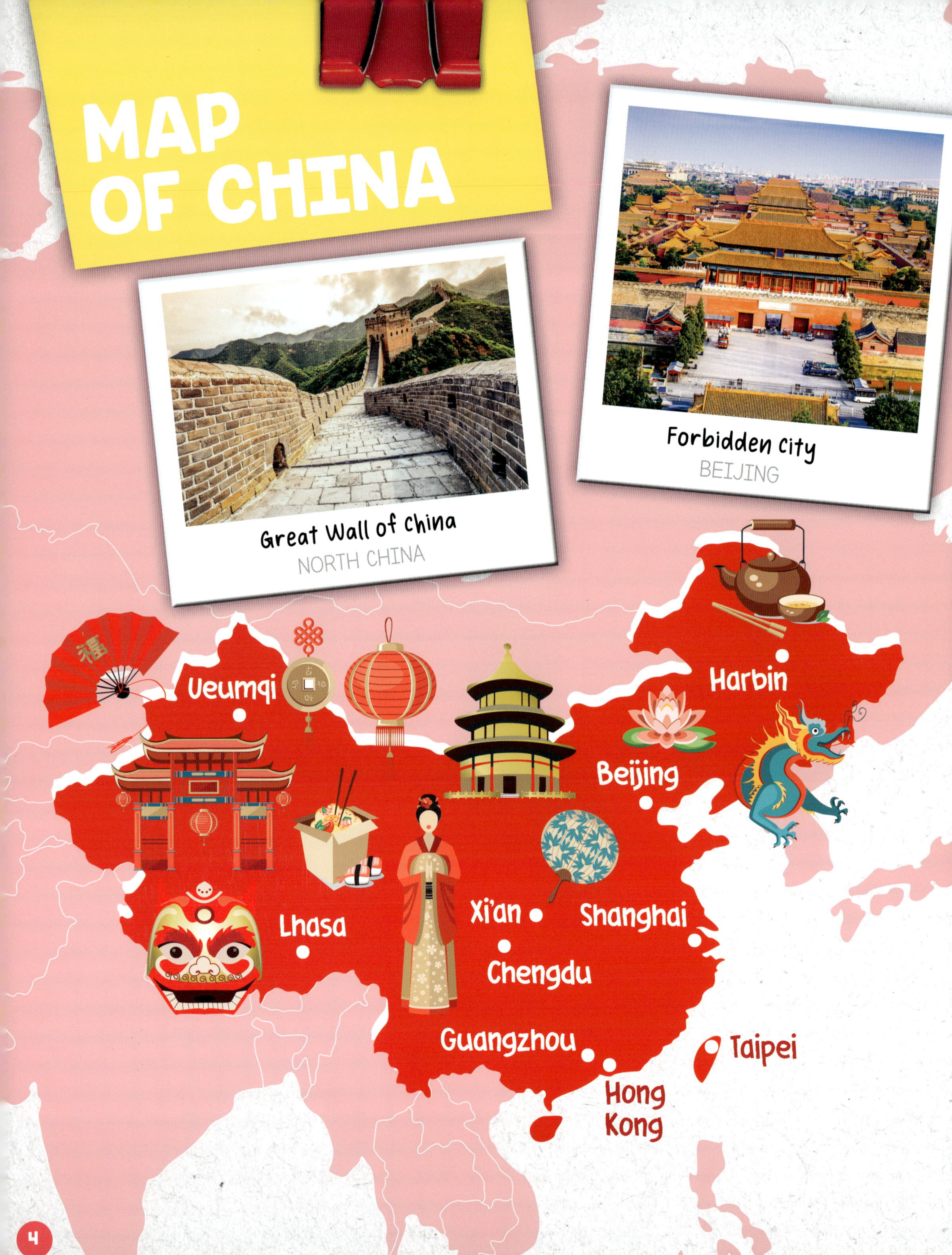

Great Wall of China
NORTH CHINA

Forbidden City
BEIJING

Terracotta Army
XIAN, SHAANXI

Huangshan
ANHUI PROVINCE

Ming Tombs
BEIJING

SNAPSHOT

COUNTRY
People's Republic of China

CAPITAL
Beijing

OFFICIAL LANGUAGE
Standard Mandarin

AREA
9,596,961 square kilometres

POPULATION
1,418,695,046 (2019)

RELIGIONS Buddhism, Taoism, Islam, Christianity

CURRENCY
元 Renminbi

GOVERNMENT
Communist state

WELCOME TO CHINA

China is the fourth largest country in the world (after Russia, Canada and the USA). It has the largest population in the world, with over 1.4 billion people.

China is a country of diversity. It has many different landscapes, unique animals, and even different climates. The people are diverse too. There are many different groups of Chinese people, called ethnic groups. Each group has its own traditions, language and customs.

Solar panels surround the city
CHONGQING

China has a vast history, dating back to 6,000 BC. The People's Republic of China was established on October 1, 1949 and, since then, has been governed by the Communist Party of China. Even though China is known for its many famous historical sites, such as the Great Wall of China, it is also a country that is investing in the future. New cities are being built, many with sustainable energy sources in place.

Five Fast Facts

1. China is the world's second largest economy and its largest trading nation.
2. It is the world's biggest producer of solar energy.
3. It produces 70 per cent of the world's mobile phones.
4. It produces 60 per cent of the world's shoes.
5. It is the world's largest producer of tea and rice.

While it is a country with a rich and complex past, it is also a global superpower and leader on the world stage.

PEOPLE

China is a diverse country with 56 recognised ethnic groups. Each group has its own religion, traditions and language.

Some of China's Ethnic Groups Include:

Han

Over 90 per cent of China's population is Han. The Han speak many different dialects but share the Mandarin writing system. Almost one in five people on the planet are Han.

Miao

There are about nine million Miao. They practise a form of spirit worship where they contact ancestors. The women wear beautiful clothes and jewellery that are handed down from generation to generation. Miao people enjoy music and many play the traditional instrument called the 'Lusheng'.

Miao people playing the Lusheng

Fun Fact

China is so big it is spread across five different time zones, but all of China follows a single standard time called Beijing Time, or China Standard Time (CST) internationally. This means that in some parts of China sunrise can be as late as 10 am.

Kam (Dong People)

There are over 2.5 million Dong people in the Southern provinces of Hunan and Guizhou. They are recognised for their unique architecture and carpentry skills. When a child is born, Dong people plant trees. Then, when that child becomes an adult, those trees are cut down and used to build that person a house.

Did You Know?

One in every five people in the world is Chinese.

Blang

Blang culture is rich in superstition and tradition. They believe their lives are ruled by ghosts and gods, and they have a rich oral tradition of stories and songs.

Chinese Teochew Opera during the Ghost Festival

Uygur (Uigur)

The Uygur are Muslim and have their own language and alphabet. They are known for their gold, silk, leather goods and gems, and they have a long history dating back to trading along the Silk Routes.

Family is the focus of daily life in China and it is common to live with two or more generations, especially in rural areas. Grandparents help care for young children, so their parents can work. In turn, the elderly are also cared for in old age, and when this can't happen, they are cared for by the state.

Life in Cities

China has 665 cities, with more being developed. Forty-one of these have a population of over two million people, while six of the cities have a population of ten million or more. Major cities like Shanghai and Beijing are modern metropolises. People often live in high-rise apartments, although as the standard of living has improved many people now live in new residential areas. The largest cities are either coastal or near the coast.

High-rise apartments
SHANGHAI

Did You Know?

Over 100 million people in China live on less than one dollar a day.

Life in Rural Areas

Over half the population still lives in towns and villages, or in the countryside. There are over 300 million farmers in China, and many of them still till the land by hand. Life in the countryside can be tough, but is very community oriented. Some places are difficult to get to, so relationships with neighbours are important.

Many people in the countryside live in two or three story houses. Most of the population lives in the eastern and central provinces of the country, on more fertile lands.

Farmer working a rice field
DALI

EDUCATION

Children in China attend primary school for six years and then high school for another six years, usually six days a week. There is a lot of pressure on many Chinese students to do well in school, so they often attend after-school tutoring if their family can afford it.

Language

There are hundreds of languages and dialects spoken in China, but China's official language is Mandarin. Written Mandarin is made up of characters rather than letters.

The order of each stroke in the character is important

SPORTS

One only needs to watch the medal tally at the Olympic Games, to know that China is a nation that takes its sports very seriously. The most popular sports are football, table tennis, badminton and basketball. The Chinese practise many sports where there is a mental and spiritual challenge as well as a physical one.

Beijing National Olympic stadium

BEIJING

In 2008, Beijing hosted the summer Olympics. China ranked number one in the medal tally with 98 medals, 48 of them gold. China has continued to dominate the medal tally at the Olympic Games.

Traditional Sports

Dragon boat racing dates back over 2,000 years and races are still held in China annually. There are many other traditional sports that are still practised in China. Some of these sports are:

- Tug-o-war
- Stilt walking
- Horse racing
- Firework catching
- Cross bow
- Shuttlecock kicking

Dragon boat racing

Martial Arts

China is famous for its martial arts. These practices were developed centuries ago as training for armies. Each style of martial arts has its own code of honour as well as the physical training. Some of the different styles found in China are:

Tai Chi: Each morning, in parks all over China, people gather to practise tai chi, a gentle form of exercise that uses slow movements with a meditative frame of mind.

Kung Fu: This is one of China's most famous sports.

Shaolin Martial Arts: This is a very famous style of martial arts based on Buddhist philosophies.

Qigong: This tests not only physical strength but includes breath techniques for the mind.

Tai Chi

Shaolin Martial Arts

Hollywood Calls

Western audiences became familiar with China's martial arts styles through the movies of champions turned actors like Bruce Lee, Jackie Chan and Jet Li.

HISTORY

China is a big country with a vast history. Civilisation began around 6,000 BC when hunter-gatherers started to plant seeds and early farming began. Around 3,000 BC, the Longshan culture built settlements, grew crops and raised animals. They were the first people to use a potter's wheel.

Dynasties

For thousands of years, China was ruled by dynasties. The Chinese believed their rulers were divinely selected. The first dynasty was the Xia. They reigned for 500 years, however what is known about them comes from ancient legends. The final dynasty was the Qing dynasty (1644–1911), which was succeeded by the Republic of China. The last emperor was Puyi, who reigned from age two and who was only five when he was forced to give up his throne.

Amazing Dynasties!

福福福福

Shang (1500–1045 BC)
Writing was invented.

Zhou (1123–256 BC)
Confucianism and Taoism spread.

Han (206 BC–220 AD)
Paper and porcelain were invented.

Tang (618–906 AD)
China had its first female emperor, Wu Chao.

Ming (1368–1644 AD)
Journey to the West was written.

Fun Fact

Toilet paper was invented in China but it was only used by emperors.

Communism

In 1911, the Qing dynasty was overthrown. The Nationalist Party declared China a republic. The Communist Party was formed and in 1949 Mao Zedong became the leader of the People's Republic of China. Chairman Mao died in 1976.

Gate of Heavenly Peace
TIANANMEN SQUARE, BEIJING

Mao Zedong

Mao was born in 1893 in Hunan Province. He was the son of a peasant, and became the leader of the Communist Party. Between 1966 and 1976, Mao made many big changes in China.

A New Era

Today, traditional Chinese culture is thriving, and the government is very supportive of the arts.

Dancers perform a folk dance
CHENGDU

While there is no official religion, Buddhism is popular in China. Other religions practised are Confucianism, Daoism and Islam. Freedom of religion is provided for in the constitution.

RELIGION AND BELIEFS

Buddhism

Buddhism is practised by more than 245 million Chinese. Most Chinese Buddhists combine both Taoist and Confucian beliefs with ancestor worship.

Christianity

Christianity arrived in China in the 7th century. Some estimates put the Christian population in China at around 100 million.

Nanputuo Buddhist temple
XIAMEN

Taoism (Daoism) 

Taoism is based on the teachings of Laozi, a 6th century BC philosopher. Other faiths and paths practised in China often include aspects of Taoism in them.

Islam 

Islam arrived in China around the middle of the 7th century AD with Arab traders and diplomats along the Silk Road. Around 24 million Muslims live in China, mostly in the northwest provinces.

Confucianism

Confucius was a philosopher who lived from 551 to 478 BC. He taught that strong family ties and respect for elders were important for society. One of his most famous sayings was, *"What you do not wish for yourself, do not do to others."* Followers reflect on their actions and how they affect others. The teachings of Confucius include five virtues:

- **Benevolence**
- 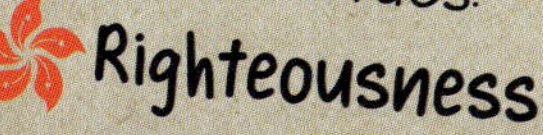 **Righteousness**
- 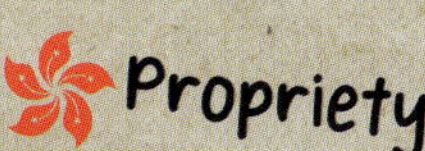 **Propriety**
- 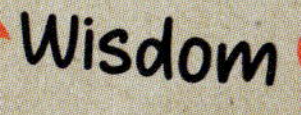 **Wisdom**
-  **Fidelity**

FOOD

Chinese food is popular in the west. It is influenced by geography, weather, and access to ingredients, making it very diverse.

If China has a national dish, then Peking duck is it. With its thin, crispy skin, Peking duck is eaten with steamed pancakes, spring onions and sweet bean sauce. Peking duck originates from Beijing.

The country can be broken into four major cuisine regions: north, south, east and west.

Northern China

Pork and chive dumplings are a favourite of this region.

Eastern China

Cooking methods include stir-fry, steaming and simmering.

Western China

Halal dishes such as roasted lamb and Lanzhou Beef Noodles are popular.

Southern China

Pork, poultry and fish dishes are preferred over lamb.

Peking Duck served with chinese pancakes

Festival Foods

China's annual calendar is packed with festivals and many come with their own delicious traditional treats. These foods symbolise different wishes and desires, such as good fortune or good health. Some of the more popular foods that people share throughout the festival year are sweet rice balls, eaten during the Lantern Festival. They are associated with families being together.

Chinese New Year

The most important event on the Chinese calendar is Chinese New Year. It is a time for celebration where family come together and eat traditional foods.

- Fruits like tangerines and oranges bring good luck and fortune if eaten over the New Year period.
- The New Year's feast for people in the north includes dumplings, while those in southern China eat sticky rice cakes.

Yum Yum!

Would you try any of these tasty treats served up in China?

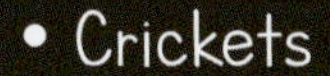

Roasted:

- Silkworm Pupae
- Seahorse
- Scorpions

Deep fried:

- Lizards
- Crickets

LANDSCAPE AND CLIMATE

China boasts some of the world's most beautiful scenery, from soaring mountains and high plateaux to vast deserts and low-lying plains and rivers.

Mountain Ranges

Nearly two-thirds of China is high mountain ranges and plateaux. China has seven of the world's twelve peaks over 8,000 metres. Well-known mountain ranges include the Kunlun Mountains, the Tianshan Mountains, the Greater Hinggan Mountains and the Taihang Mountains.

The Qinghai-Tibetan Plateau is the highest plateau in the world with an average altitude of 4,500 metres. The area also has lakes, rivers, grasslands and gorges. The Himalayas and Mount Everest straddle the border between China and Nepal.

Climate

On the Tibetan Plateau, temperatures are always low, but for most of China temperatures vary greatly depending on the region and the time of year. July is the hottest month and January is the coldest. Summers are hot and humid in the east with a monsoon climate. Most of the country's rain falls during the summer months and this can cause flooding. China experiences typhoons along the southern and eastern coast.

Yak stands in the cold temperatures

TIBETAN PLATEAU

Lowlands and Rivers

River systems like the Yellow and Yangtze have helped shape China and are important to the many people who live and farm along them. The Yangtze River is China's longest river at 6,380 kilometres.

Fishermen
YANGTZE RIVER

Did You Know?

China shares a border with 14 countries.

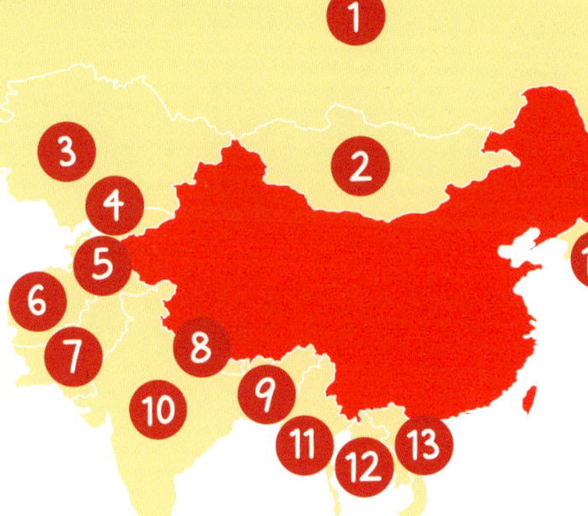

1. Russia
2. Mongolia
3. Kazakhstan
4. Kyrgyzstan
5. Tajikistan
6. Afghanistan
7. Pakistan
8. Nepal
9. Bhutan
10. India
11. Laos
12. Myanmar
13. Vietnam
14. North Korea

Deserts

Over 20 per cent of China's land area is made up of large deserts. Climate change is having an impact on these regions: deserts are expanding and drought is an increasing problem.

FABULOUS FAUNA

China has a rich array of habitats, and there is a growing trend towards environmentalism to look after them. China has incredible wildlife diversity, with ten per cent of the world's total wildlife.

There are 6,266 species of vertebrates in China, many of them unique to the country. Some of China's more unusual creatures are:

- the golden-haired monkey
- Chinese alligator
- red-crowned crane
- the white-flag dolphin
- South China tiger
- brown-eared pheasant
- red ibis

The Giant Panda

Giant pandas live in the mountains in central China. They eat leaves, stems and bamboo shoots. Unfortunately, their diet leaves them vulnerable to any loss of their habitat. Deforestation has driven the panda out of many areas. China is doing everything possible to protect the panda. In recent years, its numbers have increased and its status has been upgraded from endangered to vulnerable, but there are still only 1,864 pandas left in the wild.

China's most famous resident is the giant panda. This large black and white bear is considered a national treasure.

IMPORTANT SITES

Temple of Heaven
BEIJING

China is home to many of the world's most famous and important historical sites. Over 67 million people visit China annually, many to see these incredible sites.

The Great Wall

China's most famous destination actually stretches for over 20,000 kilometres. Parts of the wall are over 2,000 years old and in ruins. One popular part of the wall to visit, which has been restored, is north of Beijing at Mutianyu.

The Forbidden City

In the heart of Beijing is the world's largest palace complex. It was off limits for over 500 years but is now one of the country's most famous destinations.

Terracotta Warriors

Emperor Qin Shi Huang left behind some of China's most spectacular sites. During his reign, he not only started building the wall, but also a mausoleum for himself. Some 700 workers spent three decades building a compound that includes 8,000 terracotta soldiers, many with horses and chariots. Each of the terracotta warriors has its own distinct facial features.

Huangshan Mountains in the mist

HUANGSHAN DISTRICT, ANHUI

Huangshan

Huangshan in China's east is considered by many to be one of the country's most beautiful areas. Its granite peaks and mist-shrouded views have inspired many poets and artists.

ANCIENT ARTS

Chinese culture stretches back for thousands of years, with magnificent art forms developing over that time.

Music

The ancient Chinese were the first to divide instruments into categories. The categories were silk, wood, clay, hide, bamboo, gourd, metal and stone.

One form of music that has been popular for centuries is Chinese opera. Performers wear ornate costumes and face paint, and sing in high-pitched and sometimes guttural sounds. The most famous of these is the Beijing Opera. Performers require gruelling training in acrobatics, acting and singing.

Calligraphy

Decorative handwriting is considered a great art in China. Children often attend classes to learn the art of calligraphy. Chinese script is made up of over 47,000 different characters, but even highly educated people only know about three to four thousand characters.

Literature

Without the Chinese we wouldn't even have books. Papermaking was invented during the Han dynasty in 105 AD. Then, in the 11th century, the printing press was invented and book publishing began.

The oldest surviving book dates back to 868 AD, during the Tang dynasty. There is a wealth of texts from the Hundred Schools of Thought including the classics of Confucianism and Taoism.

Painting of confucius teaching
ZHANJIANG

Porcelain

Porcelain has been made and sold in China for thousands of years. Techniques for making pottery improved during the Ming Dynasty and today Ming vases are very valuable antiques.

TRANSPORT

China is a huge country with diverse geography. Modern transport systems have been built to link cities and move people and goods all around the country.

Roads

All of China's major cities and hubs have been linked by modern highways. Car ownership has risen and China is now the largest automobile market in the world. Many Chinese people continue to ride bikes.

Bicycles

Pedal power remains the favourite mode of ground transport, with more than half a billion bikes in China. While it might be the bicycle capital of the world, bikes were first introduced from the west at the end of the 19th century. Even then it took until the 1930s for the Chinese to truly embrace this mode of transport.

Did You Know?

There are over 130 million bicycles in the world. About 66 per cent of them are in China.

Railways

China has the second longest network of train tracks in the world. Trains carry goods and people across vast distances. More recently, China has built an extensive high-speed rail grid that is overlaid onto the existing railway network. China now has the most extensive high-speed rail network in the world.

The Mighty Maglev

The Maglev in Shanghai is the world's fastest train. It has achieved a Chinese record speed of 501 kilometres per hour, however its top operational commercial speed is 431 kilometres per hour.

The Silk Road

The Silk Road was a series of land and sea trade routes between China and the Mediterranean. It was established in 130 BC and was in use until the route closed in 1453 AD.

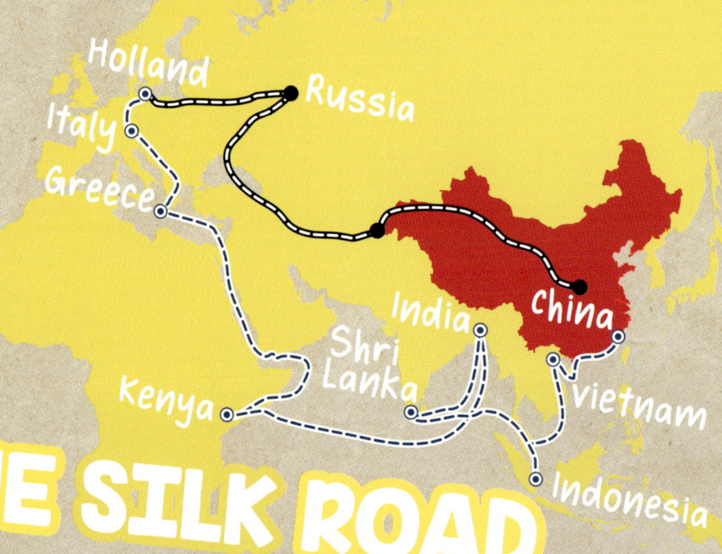

FLAG AND SYMBOLS

Flag of China

The national flag consists of one large gold star and four smaller gold stars on a red background. Each feature of the flag has symbolic meaning. Red stands for the communist revolution, and the large star symbolises the Communist Party of China.

The flag was first flown on October 1, 1949, the day the People's Republic of China was officially founded.

The four smaller stars represent the people.

The Five Elements

WATER

WOOD

FIRE

EARTH

METAL

Five is a significant number to the Chinese, because it is associated with the five elements.

The National Emblem

The National Emblem of the People's Republic of China is the same red and gold as the flag, and also contains five stars representing the Communist Party and the people. Inside a red circle is an image of Tiananmen Gate, the entrance to the Forbidden City, where Mao declared the foundation of the People's Republic of China.

National Anthem

March of the Volunteers is the national anthem of China.

Dragons

The mythical dragon is an important symbol in China.

National Animal

China's national animal is the giant panda.

GLOSSARY

Buddhism A religion based on the teachings of Buddha.

Climate change A shift in the planet's weather and climate patterns.

Communism An economic and social system where property and resources are collectively owned by a classless society and not by individual citizens.

Culture Practices, beliefs and customs of a society or people.

Delta A geographical region where a river divides into smaller rivers and empties into a larger body of water.

Dynasty A series of rulers from the same family.

Endangered When a species is at risk.

Ethnic group People who share a common culture, language and heritage.

Highlands A mountainous or elevated region.

Monsoon A season of heavy rain.

Plateau Large, flat area found in higher regions.

Sustainability Support of the environment in order to maintain an ecological balance.

Yin and Yang Two opposing principles in Chinese philosophy. Yin is feminine and yang is masculine.

Movies to Watch

- *The Karate Kid*
- *Mulan*

INDEX

Books to Read

- *Tiger* (The Five Ancestors series) by Jeff Stone
- *Dragonkeeper* by Carol Wilkinson
- *Secrets of the Terra-Cotta Soldier* by Ying Cheng Compestine